YOUR KNOWLEDGE HAS VALUE

- We will publish your bachelor's and master's thesis, essays and papers

- Your own eBook and book -
  sold worldwide in all relevant shops

- Earn money with each sale

Upload your text at www.GRIN.com
and publish for free

Bibliographic information published by the German National Library:

The German National Library lists this publication in the National Bibliography; detailed bibliographic data are available on the Internet at http://dnb.dnb.de .

This book is copyright material and must not be copied, reproduced, transferred, distributed, leased, licensed or publicly performed or used in any way except as specifically permitted in writing by the publishers, as allowed under the terms and conditions under which it was purchased or as strictly permitted by applicable copyright law. Any unauthorized distribution or use of this text may be a direct infringement of the author s and publisher s rights and those responsible may be liable in law accordingly.

Imprint:

Copyright © 2018 GRIN Verlag
Print and binding: Books on Demand GmbH, Norderstedt Germany
ISBN: 9783668713000

This book at GRIN:

https://www.grin.com/document/427081

Caroline Mutuku

The Duality of Nationalism. Example Korea

GRIN Verlag

GRIN - Your knowledge has value

Since its foundation in 1998, GRIN has specialized in publishing academic texts by students, college teachers and other academics as e-book and printed book. The website www.grin.com is an ideal platform for presenting term papers, final papers, scientific essays, dissertations and specialist books.

Visit us on the internet:

http://www.grin.com/

http://www.facebook.com/grincom

http://www.twitter.com/grin_com

Nationalism Is a Double-Edged Sword

Nationalism has been compared to a double edged sword because it either be a blessing, and consequently unite the people, or it can be a curse because of its divisive capability. Nationalism preys on the emotive aspiration of a community or an ethnic group. In Korea, nationalism has had much to do with the nations turbulent past as well as the years of modern transformation when it was used as force anti-colonialism and modernization (Gi-Wook 17). Today, it is still a source of pride and inspiration for many Koreans and still functions as a important ideological anchor for national unification of the divided Korea. On the other hand, nationalism has exacted a heavy toll to the Korean society in terms o their culture and political development. Many scholars hold the opinion that it has marginalized many competing voices in the name of the immortal nation as well as being a weapon of suppressing the civic rights and the freedom of the citizens. Korea is still battling with the task of transforming the national identity which is based on common ancestry into a cohesive democratic identity (Gi-Wook 18).

There is a strong tradition that pervades the scholarship of nationalism. The tradition takes the view that political nationalism is civic, constructive, and integrative while ethnic nationalism is dangerous, destructive, and divisive. Consequently, ethnic cleavages are seen as more fundamental, and, therefore, permanent that other types of cleavage. The conflict that arise from ethnic nationalism is the most difficult to sort out. Some scholars have opined that ethically driven conflicts are intrinsically untenable to compromise than the type of nationalism that revolves round material interests. The scholars argue that the ethnic nationalism revolve around particular symbols as well as specific conceptions of legitimacy while being characterized by several competing demands that cannot be divided into bargainable items.

However, according to Gi-Wook, such a view overlooks the complexity and diversity of the role of ethnic nationalism. For instance, some scholars have argued that in Japan, ethnic nationalism has functioned as a significant form of populist attack on the government that was seen as authoritarian. The ethnic nationalism overshadowed the civic society. The scholars further argue that the modern liberal state has not overcome the notion of the fatherland. In Germany, after the Berlin wall came down, ethnic nationalism was stoked by the state as a potentially unifying force. When the state was faced by the difficult process of reunification, the elites employed ethnic nationalism as one of the strategy to lure the people to meet the cost of the delegitimized East Germany and the apolitical West Germany. Consequently, the prevailing slogans shifted from the cry "we are the people" to "we are one people" (Gi-Wook 15). The superficial appeal to nationalism illustrates the complexity of ethnic nationalism that is overlooked in the modern literature on nationalism.

In the Korean situation, the question has often been whether nationalism is helpful, and whether it should be viewed as an ideology of resistance or one of domination. However, there are certain studies that have pointed out some dark and fascist side of the Korean nationalism, regardless, the prevailing perspective continue to cast it positively, primarily as an ideology of anti-colonialism and national unification. The Korean history of nationalism is closely associated with the regime legitimacy with each side of the political divide patronizing its version of nationalist narratives, and yet, the double-edged characteristic of nationalism must be recognized since it can easily be both a curse and a blessing.

The rise of nationalistic feelings is a blessing for the individuals who share a common language, history, and culture, but without a nation-state. For instance, when Korea was occupied by Japanese, the feeling of nationalism bound the people together. They had common interests to protect from the colonizers. On the other hand, the nationalism liberating potential can easily be converted to the rationale for domination, intolerance, persecution and repression as happened in post-colonial Korea, especially before the democratic transition in 1947 (Gi-Wook 15).

Suffice to say, nationalism is a fairly harmless phenomenon, however, when it is combined with other ideological inclination, its effect can be devastating. Some scholars have correctly pointed out that nationalism allows for camouflaged permutation because it can easily be combined with other ideologies such as racism, liberalism, and romanticism, to serve a variety of objectives from authoritarian to democratic, unifying to divisive, anti-modern to modern. Korea has witnessed different forms of ideologies from communism to capitalism as well as agrarianism, authoritarian, and democracy (Gi-Wook 16). The state was also was exposed to local as well as global forces. The ethnic nationalism phenomena have been credited with the escalating conflicts between the North and South Korea and at the same time serving as an ideology for national unification. That is the contradictory nature of nationalism. As the Korean scholars grapple with the complex nature of nationalism, they should also recognize its dual aspect and recognize the effect it has had on the political development of the Korean people (Gi-Wook 18).

Korea had a different experience of nationalism from other nation in the world, even with the countries that are compared with Korea, such as Japan and Germany. Its experience is useful in delineating and understanding the complexity of nationalism. For instance, West European and African states adopted a territorial notion of nation-state and ethnicity was suppressed by the nation building efforts. However, in Korea ethnicity has been a major element in the formulation of national identity (Gi-Wook 18). The state has maintained a coherent and vibrant political community in a stable territorial boundary run by an established agrarian bureaucracy. Most importantly, Korea has maintained a fairly homogenous ethnic or historical nation for many centuries. The historical experiences can be contrasted with that o Western Europe where the current boundaries and political map was only formed in the modern era. These countries nationalism is anchored on political ideology and fostered in order to integrate the diverse ethnic groups into a relatively coherent political community or the nation. Although Korea has been divided into two states since 1945, its one ethnic nation divided into two states characteristic is a unique phenomenon since other nations have many ethnic groups brought together by the national boundaries to form a nation (Gi-Wook 19). Another difference between Korea and most nations that were colonized, Korea was only assimilated to the larger Japanese empire. Thus, it was able to maintain its land, language, and culture. It is a common ancestry and shared blood notion that drove Korea's anti-colonialism nationalism during the japans occupation.

Some scholars have opined that globalization is the formation of a borderless world with weak nation-state regimes, the Koreas case is different. The government played a significant role in when it deliberately initiated the managed globalization policy. Globalization became an ideology and state policy during the reign of Kim Young Sam between 1993 and 1998 (Gi-Wook 205). In what became known as the Sydney Declaration, the President, using the increased global competition in a fast globalizing world, announced the government drive and desire for globalization in order to meet the rapidly evolving conditions in the world economy. Thus, the government took deliberate steps to prepare for Koreas position in a globalized world. A Globalization Promotion Committee was set up to oversee the globalization process. The government initiative was again different from the other nations since the globalization phenomena was driven by private enterprises and not deliberate state policy (Gi-Wook 206). Suffice to say, the globalization phenomena have a different meaning in Korea from the understanding of the western world. The Korean states do not suffer from the envisaged weakened nations as a result of globalization because the Korean nation is grounded on ancestry and shared birthrights. The Korean nation is the people of Korea.

Recent arguments on globalization and nationalism have centered on the question whether globalization will render the function of nation-states weak or whether the national culture and identity will be replaced by the global culture and cosmopolitan identity. Some scholars contend that the regulatory leverage held by states will disappear because of the free cross-border activities in commerce and trade through imitation, competition, capital mobility, and diffusion of best practices, thus, creating a divergence across nations in structures of production and the relationships between the society, economy and state (Gi-Wook 19 221). The advocates of this theory conclude that the state guided by nationalism as the basic ideology has outlived its usefulness in the management of the world order. However, a number o scholars and policy makers have dismissed the notion of the demise of the nation-states because the globalization phenomenon is not unprecedented and the nation state cannot disappear, however, they concede that it would have to change it functional role. The states will play a proactive role in managing and shaping the globalization process, accommodate the global flow, and ultimately turn such forces its national interest (Gi-Wook 8). It is possible that instead of weakening national and ethnic identities it will intensify them.

The problems that are immanent to nationalism in Korea are associated with the concept of *minjok* or the Korean nation. The reason for the obscurity in the definition of *minjok* lies in its etymological formation of the term (de Wit 24). The terminology does not seem to bear a clear definition. *Min* means the people while *jok* means the family. The two words stretch back to the classical age. The meaning of the two characters can only be comprehended in the context they are applied and in association with other entities in the statement. The concept of *minjok* is used to rally nationalism in defense of the Korean nation and strengthen national unity. Thus, the bloodline of the ethnic nation is associated with the *minjok* to imply that the nation had an identifiable spiritual essence that has remained intact for al long time. Therefore, although Korea has been divided into two countries, the Korean people continue to think of themselves as one people. The problem is further acerbated by the ideological orientation of the two Korean states (de Wit 25).

The globalization perspective does not contradict the local perspective. Just as Gi-wook (2006) argues, the global can be appropriated for local interests. Thus, globalization, like its predecessor modernization, can be proactively used as a means to enhance local interests out of choice or necessity. The modern Asian history is replete with examples of countries that have appropriated the global forces for their national interests (Gi-Wook 222). The Asia countries, such as Japan, china, and Korea have appropriated Western technologies and science even as they were being encroached by imperialism. The instrumentalist concept of modernization prevailed during the state of Korea drive to modernize the fatherland. The recent proactive efforts in globalization in Korea can be seen in the same light. It is an effort to increase Korea's national competitiveness in a rapidly expanding market, and underpinned by the continuing advances in communications technologies. The government has been on the frontline in promoting Koreas values and culture in order to preserve the nation as the influence of globalization threaten to engulf the nation. However, there is no indication that either the national or the global forces will replace each other or disappear in the future. The most likely scenario is that both forces will find equilibrium in order to co-exist and complement each other.

Thus, globalization reinforces the development of the national interest and fosters the unique national characteristic of the Korean nation (Gi-Wook 224).

To sum up, although nationalism has been compared to a double edged sword, the case of Korea is unique and the sentiment may not entirely describe the Korean situation. Korea historical evolvement and development has cast its brand of nationalism in different colors from the rest of the world. Korea is the only state that has taken deliberate steps to anticipate and prepare for the effects of globalization and its expected pervasive influence.

Work cited

de Wit, Jerôme. *The Dilemmas of Nationalism during Civil War*, 2010. Web: http://www.koreanhistories.org/files/Volume_2_2/KH2_2_De_Wit_Dilemmas.pdf

Gi-Wook, Shin. *Ethnic Nationalism in Korea*. Stanford: Stanford University Press. 2006. Print.

YOUR KNOWLEDGE HAS VALUE

- We will publish your bachelor's and master's thesis, essays and papers

- Your own eBook and book - sold worldwide in all relevant shops

- Earn money with each sale

Upload your text at www.GRIN.com and publish for free